On Longevity and Shortness of Life

*Aristotle's Study of the
Secrets of a Long Life*

A Modern Translation

Adapted for the Contemporary Reader

Aristotle

© Copyright 2025. All rights reserved.

It is not legal to reproduce, duplicate, or transmit any part of this document in either electronic means or in printed format. Recording of this publication is strictly prohibited and any storage of this document is not allowed unless with written permission from the publisher except for the use of brief quotations in a book review.

Table of Contents

Preface - Message to the Reader 1
Introduction 3
On Longevity and Shortness of Life 12
Thank you for Reading 23

Preface - Message to the Reader

Rebuilding the Greatest Library in Human History

Thousands of years ago, the Library of Alexandria was the heart of global knowledge — a sanctuary where the wisdom of every known civilization was gathered and shared freely.

And then, it was lost.

Now, we're rebuilding it — and you are invited to join us.

At the Library of Alexandria, we've set out to make every book available to *every person on Earth* — not just in print, but in every language, every format, and for every reader.

Here's how we do it:

- **Deluxe Print Editions at True Printing Cost** - Order any book as a high-quality paperback, elegant hardcover, or stunning boxset — and only pay what it costs to print. No markups. No middlemen.

- **Unlimited Access to the Greatest Works** - Enjoy thousands of timeless classics — from Plato to Shakespeare to Tolstoy — in beautiful, modern eBook and audiobook editions. Read and listen without limits — for every reader, everywhere.

- **Modern Translations for Every Language & Dialect** - We're reimagining the classics in clear, accessible language — and translating them into every dialect imaginable. Everyone deserves to understand humanity's greatest ideas.

When you visit **LibraryofAlexandria.com**, you're not just accessing books — you're joining a global movement to restore, preserve, and share the wisdom of civilization.

Join us today at LibraryofAlexandria.com

Together, we'll ensure the light of human wisdom never fades again.

With gratitude,
The Modern Library of Alexandria Team

Visit:
www.libraryofalexandria.com

Or scan the code below:

Introduction

Ancient Greece was a civilization famous for its great contributions to philosophy, politics, art, and science. It thrived from the 8th century BCE until the Roman Empire started to decline. Greece's city-states, especially Athens, were the heart of culture and intellectual thought. This was the time when democracy began, impressive buildings like the Parthenon were built, and famous playwrights like Sophocles and Euripides produced their works. The Greeks' curiosity about the world around them laid the foundation for Western philosophy. Thinkers like Socrates, Plato, and later Aristotle, pushed the limits of what people understood about the world.

Greek society was deeply connected to theism, which focused on a large group of gods and goddesses who were believed to control every part of life. But this system did not prevent people from exploring new ideas. In fact, it coexisted with a growing interest in finding logical explanations for nature and human life. Intellectuals would often debate and discuss these ideas in public places like the Agora. Aristotle grew up in this dynamic environment, learning from earlier philosophers, and later challenging and expanding their ideas.

Aristotle's Life

Aristotle was born in 384 BCE in a small town called Stagira, located in northern Greece. His father, Nicomachus, was a doctor for King Amyntas of Macedon, and this allowed Aristotle to be around the Macedonian royal court from a young age. When his parents passed away, Aristotle was sent to Athens at the age of 17 to pursue his education. Athens was the center of intellectual life in Greece, and Aristotle joined Plato's Academy, which was the most respected school of the time. The Academy was a place where students discussed everything from ethics to science. Although Aristotle learned a lot from Plato, he did not always agree with him, especially when it came to metaphysics, which deals with the nature of reality.

After spending almost 20 years at the Academy, Aristotle left Athens around 347 BCE after Plato's death. He traveled around different cities in Greece, continuing to study and learn. In 343 BCE, he was invited to the court of King Philip II of Macedon, where he became the tutor of Philip's son, Alexander, who would later become known as Alexander the Great. Aristotle taught Alexander about philosophy, ethics, politics, and science. Aristotle's influence is visible in Alexander's leadership style, which showed respect for knowledge and strategic thinking.

After teaching Alexander, Aristotle returned to Athens in 335 BCE, where he opened his own school called the Lyceum. Unlike Plato's Academy, the Lyceum focused more on recording knowledge and observing nature. Aristotle and his students performed research, studied animals, and took notes on what they observed. The Lyceum became a major center of learning, and it rivaled Plato's Academy. This is also where Aristotle wrote many of his famous works.

Later in life, after the death of Alexander in 323 BCE, the political climate in Athens became difficult for Aristotle because of his connections to the Macedonian court. Accused of disrespecting the gods, Aristotle decided to leave Athens. He fled to Chalcis, where he passed away in 322 BCE. Even though he had to leave Athens, his legacy lived on through his many writings and the influence of his school, the Lyceum.

Aristotle's Impact on Western Thought

No figure looms larger over the development of Western philosophy and science than Aristotle. A student of Plato and tutor to Alexander the Great, he unified logic, ethics, politics, rhetoric, and metaphysics into a coherent system that shaped intellectual inquiry for centuries. Although his writings reflect the best knowledge of his era, they also reveal a distinctive way of understanding the world—one that balances observation with rigorous logical analysis. Over time, this method has profoundly influenced everything from political theory to modern scientific methodology.

Aristotle approached knowledge as an interconnected whole, seeing each field of study as a vital path toward truth. While many earlier thinkers focused on abstract concepts, he emphasized direct observation of the natural world. By systematically examining and classifying what he saw, Aristotle laid the groundwork for the empirical methods now central to modern science. Although our understanding of nature has evolved, his legacy endures in today's emphasis on evidence-based research.

Logic: The Foundation of Rational Inquiry

Often hailed as the "father of formal logic," Aristotle introduced a system of reasoning that shaped intellectual discourse for over two millennia. In works like the Organon, he analyzed how valid conclusions are drawn from premises and introduced syllogisms—deductive arguments that became standard tools in philosophy, theology, and science. Even contemporary logic, despite its modern mathematical and symbolic advancements, can trace many of its core principles back to Aristotle's pioneering analyses.

Metaphysics: Exploring the Nature of Reality

Aristotle's Metaphysics offered one of the earliest comprehensive explorations of existence at its most fundamental level. There, he described the nature of "being qua being" and introduced the concepts of potentiality and actuality to explain how things change and develop. These ideas deeply influenced medieval scholastics—both Christian and Islamic—who integrated Aristotelian reasoning into their theological frameworks. Today, discussions about consciousness, identity, and free will still reference these Aristotelian notions.

Ethics and the Pursuit of the Good Life

In the Nicomachean Ethics, Aristotle proposed that the ultimate aim of human life is eudaimonia, often translated as "happiness" or "flourishing." He argued that we achieve this through virtue, developed by cultivating good habits guided by reason. His famous Doctrine of the Mean asserts that moral virtue resides between two extremes—for instance, courage lies between recklessness and cowardice. This focus on character formation has profoundly shaped the tradition known as "virtue ethics," influencing modern debates on moral education, personal development, and what it means to live well.

Politics: The Role of the Individual in the City-State

Aristotle's practical approach to ethics naturally extended into political theory. In Politics, he explored various forms of government—monarchy, aristocracy, oligarchy, democracy—and weighed their merits and pitfalls. For Aristotle, a well-ordered polis (city-state) exists not merely for survival or trade but to enable its citizens to live virtuous, fulfilling lives. His conviction that ethics and politics are intertwined remains influential, informing contemporary discussions on citizenship, governance, and justice.

Rhetoric: The Art of Persuasion

In his treatise Rhetoric, Aristotle examined how persuasion works, detailing how arguments must appeal to ethos (credibility), pathos (emotion), and logos (logic). This clear framework for effective communication continues to guide public speakers, legal advocates, and writers. From ancient courtroom orations to modern political campaigns, Aristotelian rhetoric underpins many of the strategies people use to sway audiences and shape public opinion.

Beyond these core subjects, Aristotle made significant contributions to biology, physics, psychology, and aesthetics. In the Poetics, for example, he investigated why humans respond so powerfully to tragic drama, pioneering the concept of catharsis—the emotional release that audiences feel through art. Throughout the medieval period, thinkers like Thomas Aquinas integrated Aristotle's theories into Christian theology, while Islamic philosophers such as Avicenna and Averroes preserved, interpreted, and expanded upon his works.

Across centuries of reinterpretation and debate, Aristotle remains a living voice in contemporary thought. His insistence on systematically gathering evidence and connecting it to logical principles laid the foundation for what we now recognize as the scientific method. His inquiries into human flourishing, civic responsibility, and the nature of argument continue to spark discussion and inspire new research. From personal ethics to societal organization, Aristotle's ideas help us frame enduring questions about how best to live, learn, and understand reality.

In sum, Aristotle stands as a foundational pillar of Western thought. He bridged abstract theorizing and practical inquiry, bequeathing a vision of knowledge that values both reason and experience. From ethics and politics to science and art, his ideas have been woven into countless intellectual traditions. Even today, as we grapple with questions of morality, governance, and truth, we walk in the footsteps of an ancient thinker whose breadth of insight and depth of analysis continue to guide our pursuit of wisdom.

Final Thoughts

By preserving Aristotle's legacy, we protect the intellectual depth and rigor that defined his way of understanding the world. His systematic way of asking questions, his classification of knowledge, and his ethical theories are still relevant today, providing a model for critical thinking across many subjects. This preservation is important not just for philosophy students but for anyone interested in the foundations of human thought and the development of ideas that shape the world we live in.

One of the difficulties in studying Aristotle's work is that his ideas and language are complex. Translating these works into our modern language is a key step in making his profound insights easier for more people to understand. By putting his ideas into today's language, more readers can engage with his thoughts, even if they don't have a background in classical studies. Making Aristotle's work accessible means adapting them to modern ways of thinking without losing their original depth. This helps bridge the gap between ancient and modern readers, making sure Aristotle's work stays relevant.

On Longevity and Shortness of Life

We need to investigate why some animals live long lives while others have short ones, and what causes the length or shortness of life.

To start, we need to ask whether animals and plants all have the same reason for living longer or shorter lives, or if the reasons are different. Some plants also live a long time, while others only last for a year.

Also, we should ask whether a long life and being healthy always go together, or if it's possible to live a short life but still be healthy. In some cases, disease and a short life may go hand in hand, but in others, poor health might not prevent a long life.

We've already talked about sleep and waking, and later we'll talk about life and death, and health and disease, where it makes sense to do so in the study of nature. For now, we're focusing on why some creatures live longer and others live shorter lives. This difference shows up not only between whole groups of animals, but also between individuals of the same species. For example, humans live longer than horses, but even among humans, some live longer than others. The place where people live also matters—people in warm climates tend to live longer, while those in cold climates often live shorter lives. There are also differences between individuals living in the same area.

To figure this out, we need to first answer the question: What makes some natural things easy to destroy and others not? Fire and water, and things related to them, don't have the same effects—they cause both the creation and destruction of things. So, it makes sense that everything made from fire and water would share these qualities, as long as they aren't just simple combinations of things like a house.

In other cases, the way things break down is unique to them. For example, knowledge, health, and disease disappear even though the thing they're found in (like the body or the mind) isn't destroyed. For instance, ignorance is replaced by learning or remembering, while knowledge turns into forgetfulness or error. But when a living thing dies, the health or knowledge it had also disappears. This can help us think about the soul, too. If the soul's connection to the body were like knowledge's connection to the mind, then it would have a different way of breaking down. But since the soul doesn't have this kind of connection, its relationship with the body must be different.

Some people might ask if there's a place where things that usually die, like fire, can't be destroyed, like in the upper regions of the sky where there's no opposite force. Opposites destroy each other, and through this destruction, the things connected to them are also destroyed. But if something has no opposite, or is in a place where its opposite can't reach it, it can't be destroyed. However, this isn't always true, because anything that contains matter will have some kind of opposite. For example, heat and straightness can be present in every part of something, but nothing can be only hot or straight. If that were possible, then qualities like heat or straightness would exist on their own, which they don't. And when something has both active and passive qualities, one will always affect the other, causing change. Waste, which is left over from these changes, can also act as an opposite and cause destruction.

A smaller flame can be burned up by a larger one because the smaller one uses up its fuel slowly, while the bigger one burns it up quickly.

This means that all things are constantly changing, being created, and being destroyed. Their environment can help or harm them, making them last longer or shorter than they naturally would. But nothing can live forever when it has opposite qualities, because these opposites cause things to change their location, size, or qualities over time.

We can see that neither the biggest animals nor the smallest ones are the most resistant to decay. For example, horses live shorter lives than humans, and many insects only live for a year. The same goes for plants—some only last a year. Bloodless animals don't live the longest either. For example, bees live longer than some animals with blood, even though they don't have any. And animals that live on land don't live longer than sea creatures. Crabs and mollusks, for example, don't live long lives, despite living in the sea.

Generally, the longest-lived things are plants, like the date palm. Next come animals with blood, especially those with legs. For example, humans and elephants are among the longest-lived animals. Usually, bigger animals live longer than smaller ones, as most long-lived animals are also large, like the ones I just mentioned.

Now, let's look at the reasons behind these facts. Animals are naturally warm and moist, and staying alive depends on keeping this balance. Old age, however, is dry and cold, like a dead body. You can see this with your own eyes. The bodies of all living things are made of four basic elements: hot, cold, dry, and moist. So, as things age, they must become dry. This explains why fat things don't decay as easily. Fat contains air, which is like fire, and fire doesn't break down easily.

Also, animals need a lot of moisture to stay alive. A small amount of moisture dries up quickly, which is why both large plants and animals usually live longer than smaller ones, as I mentioned earlier. It's not just the amount of moisture that matters, though. The quality of the moisture is also important. It must be both plentiful and warm so that it doesn't freeze or dry up too easily.

This is why humans live longer than some larger animals. Even though humans may have less moisture, the quality of their moisture makes up for the smaller amount.

In some animals, fat helps prevent drying out and freezing, while in others, the moisture has a different quality. Also, things that don't produce much waste live longer. Waste can cause disease or death because it weakens the body. Animals that produce a lot of waste or seed tend to age quickly. Seed is a type of residue, and losing it makes the body drier. This is why mules live longer than horses or donkeys, and why females often live longer than males, especially in species where males are very sexual. For example, male sparrows have shorter lives than females. Males who do a lot of hard work also live shorter lives because hard work causes dryness, and old age is dry. But generally, males live longer than females because males have more natural warmth.

Animals in warm climates also live longer than those in cold climates for the same reason. Warmth helps them grow larger and live longer. In cold places, the moisture in animals is more watery and freezes easily, which prevents growth. This is why cold-blooded animals like snakes and lizards grow larger in warm places. Even sea creatures like shellfish grow larger in the warm waters of the Red Sea. Warm moisture in these areas helps them both grow and live longer. But in cold areas, animals are smaller and have shorter lives because the cold freezes their moisture.

Both plants and animals will die if they aren't fed, because they will use up their own body's resources. It's like a small flame being burned up by a larger one that uses all the fuel. The natural warmth in an animal's body, which helps with digestion, will consume the materials in the body if there's no food to replace it.

Sea creatures live shorter lives than land animals, not just because they are moist, but because their moisture is watery, which is cold and easily frozen. For the same reason, bloodless animals die easily unless they are large. They don't have fat or sweetness in their bodies. Fat is sweet in animals, which is why bees live longer than some larger animals.

Plants tend to live longer than animals. This is because they have less water, so they don't freeze as easily. Also, plants have a certain oiliness and thickness that helps them hold onto moisture without drying out, even though they are naturally dry and earthy.

We need to understand why trees can last so long, as this is unique to them and not seen in animals, except in some insects.

Plants constantly renew themselves, which is why they can live for a long time. New shoots keep growing while the older parts age. The same thing happens with the roots. But these changes don't happen at the same time. First, the trunk and branches die, and new ones grow beside them. Then, when that happens, new roots grow from the surviving part of the plant. This cycle continues—one part dies while another grows—allowing the plant to live a long life.

There's a similarity between plants and insects, as mentioned before. Both can continue living even after being divided, and one can become two or more. However, insects, though they can survive after being divided, don't live for long because they don't have the organs needed to sustain life, and the separated parts can't develop new organs. In plants, each part has the potential to grow both roots and a stem. This allows plants to keep growing, with one part renewing while another part grows old, giving them a longer life. A similar process happens when you take a cutting from a plant. The cutting is part of the plant, and it can continue to live and grow even though it's no longer attached. In the case of plants, this ongoing renewal is what keeps them alive for so long. The reason for this is that the life force of the plant is present in every part of it.

The same kind of things happen in both plants and animals. In animals, males generally live longer. Males have larger upper bodies compared to their lower bodies (making them more compact or stocky than females), and the upper body is where warmth is found, while the lower body is cooler. In plants, those that have large root systems, like trees, also live longer. In plants, the roots are like the head or the upper part, and annual plants, which only live for a year, grow more in their lower parts and produce fruit.

We'll look at these things more deeply when we discuss plants specifically. But this explains why some animals live longer lives and others have shorter ones. Next, we'll explore youth, old age, life, and death. Understanding these topics will complete our study of animals.

∴

The End

Thank you for Reading

You've Just Read a Piece of the Greatest Library Ever Rebuilt

Thank you for reading.

This book is one of thousands we're restoring, reimagining, and translating as part of the **Modern Library of Alexandria** — a global movement to preserve and share humanity's most important ideas.

What was once lost to fire and time is now rising again — not just as memory, but as living, breathing knowledge, freely accessible to all.

What You Can Do Next:

- **Keep Reading.**

    Discover more legendary works — in beautiful print, audiobook, or digital form — at LibraryofAlexandria.com.

- **Build Your Own Library.**

    Every title is available as a paperback, hardcover, or collectible boxset — at true printing cost. Craft a personal library worthy of display.

- **Spread the Light.**

    Share this book. Tell others about the movement. Help us translate every timeless work into every language, so no reader is ever left behind.

By finishing this book, you've already taken part in something extraordinary.

Join us at LibraryofAlexandria.com

Together, we're rebuilding the greatest library the world has ever known.

With appreciation,
The Modern Library of Alexandria Team

Visit:

www.libraryofalexandria.com

Or scan the code below:

www.ingramcontent.com/pod-product-compliance
Lightning Source LLC
LaVergne TN
LVHW030632080426
835512LV00021B/3470